# STORMS VERSES

## When Storms Cast Spells

JOY

*To the gods of ink and thunder,*

*who carved chaos into my veins and dared me to sing.*

*To the wanderers of shadowed paths,*

*who bleed quietly into their art,*

*may these verses remind you: you're not alone in the dark.*

# Contents

# Synopsis

*Storm's Verses* is more than a poetry collection — it is a myth told in fragments, a cosmic tale whispered through stardust and silence. Across eight thematic ACTs, this collection leads the reader through a universe sculpted by ink, haunted by illusions, and bound by a fate far older than time.

Each poem is a shard of a larger, secret language — some soft and soulful, others wild as war cries or cold as stars. Rooted in themes of cosmic origins, inner dualities, ancient enchantments, forgotten lore, and haunting endings, the verses echo with both intimacy and infinity.

The journey begins with *ACT I: The Origin of Wonder,* where poetic consciousness is born — not merely human, but starlit, as if ink itself was carved from the edge of the cosmos. It then spirals into *The Dreamer's Mirage*, where perception is shattered and memory becomes a maze. The reader slips through realities like mirrors, doubting every reflection and even themselves.

As the acts unfold, emotions are peeled raw in *The Mirror of Emotion*, while spells, riddles, and riddled magic reawaken in *The Mystic Realms*. In *Lore, Legends, and War*, the tone swells into high fantasy — kingdoms fall, dragons dream in binary, and prophecy begins to stir.

Then, in the eye of the storm, *Love, Light & Quiet Bonds* offer brief warmth — a reminder of the soul's quiet corners. But the storm isn't over. Another ACT, *The Curtain Call – Illusions & Beyond*, confronts the inevitable: death, endings, and truths buried in poetic hallucinations. Far beyond everything, lies the Final ACT, *The Stormbound Prophecy*. Here, Noctherin — an original language created for the collection — speaks its darkest verses in a cursed finale poem titled **"The Verse of the Storm"**, a prophecy that binds the poet's essence to the stars, blood, and ink itself.

*Storm's Verses* is a poetic odyssey written by JOY— the alter ego of a dreamer, a coder of metaphors, and a seer of emotional storms. It reads like an ancient manuscript fallen from another realm, each stanza a spell, each act a part of a myth long forgotten… until now.

This book doesn't just want to be read.
It wants to be remembered.
And above all — it wants to return.

# ACT I

◆

## The Origin of Wonder

# 1

# Before the Stars, the Storm

Not born of stars, but of the Storm that taught them how to burn,
Cursed to wander creation, where no holy gods ever return.

~JOY

# 2

# Cosmic Child

Born as a dust cloud,
Scattered and uneven,
My particles roamed,
Lost in the cosmic reign.
For an infinity, they wandered, weightless, aimless,
Until something pulled them close-
A stellar pull, invisible,
Collected them for a mission.

They became… not me, but a star.
A giant blaze, a gas-borne fire,
Burning, waiting, doing nothing,
Trapped in the slow rhythm of celestial time.
My particles, trapped in light,
Endured the bake and the forge,

Until they knew the temperature of rebirth,
Melding like metals in the heart of a star.

Then-unexpectedly-
The star died.
With its end, I began,
My dust again freed to roam, scattered anew,
Started to explore every inch of the fabric,
The fabric of the space-time,
Across millions of lightyears,
Becoming a melody of silence and anticipation.

My dust, again, was pulled,
Fortunately not inside of a star,
But a disk made around it of other friendly dust.
Without much wait-
Just after 50 million years or something,
They became a planet,
I found myself again on.
In the dance of elements: Oxygen, carbon,
hydrogen,
Nitrogen, calcium, and phosphorus,
Blending, fusing, piecing me whole.
Some of them belonged to only me,
Those rare, singular atoms,
Their sole purpose to find each other,
Across 4.6 billion years.

And here they are, here I am,
Writing their journey as mine,
The dust cloud, the pull, the fireball, the dying,
The rebirth-
It was always meant to be,
The tale of how I became… me.

Me. The cosmic child,
Created piece by piece,
From the embers of fires forgotten.
Those stars, my ancestors,
I carry their spark in my veins,
Their end, their rise, their flame,
All burning within me, like an eternal chain.

I am a part of them-
A whisper of nebulae,
A shard of supernova's roar,
Forged into this rare form.
I am the cosmic child,
Plucked from the endless cosmic realm,
Sewn into this fabric of existence,
And sent to this planet,
Which, in its own way, feels like my sibling.

~JOY

## *Whispers from the Storm*

Humans are tiny compared to the huge universe we live in. We live in cities, situated in countries, which are part of continents, on one of the eight planets in our solar system. Our solar system is just one among countless others in the Milky Way galaxy, which itself is part of a local group within a supercluster, all nestled inside the observable universe. This perspective might feel overwhelming, but it doesn't stop us from being endlessly innovative, creating and inventing new things.

No matter how small we are in comparison to the universe, we share something very important with everything around us: we are all made of *stardust*. The very atoms in our bodies once came from stars, making us siblings to the *Earth* and all *celestial bodies*.

This poem was born from a quiet evening when I realized this beautiful truth. It reminds us that every atom in us took billions of years to become who *we* are today.

# 3

# Palette of Silence

Flowing from nebular sparks,
Made of seven vibrant marks.
White, the colour of serene light,
Speaks so little; hears the night.

Flooding cosmic realms afar,
Eating hues of every star.
Black, the shade of hidden lore?
Reveals, but hides much more.

Together, twisting and turning,
Their meld is always rising.
Black skies and white stars shining,
Different, but seems coinciding.

Palette of silence, speaks a lot,
Feels like a blessing we have got.
Like Pandas or Zebras' Beauty,
World's balance, their utmost duty.

~JOY

# *Whispers from the Storm*

Palette of silence has only two colors; Black and White. While black seems heavily mysterious and gives a feeling of darkness and negativity white does the opposite by being the sign of peace and calmness often giving the feeling of clarity and positivity.

This poem was penned for a purpose. The purpose was to make people understand the significance of these colors. How white, the color of peace is made from the seven colors of a rainbow, and black, the color of mystery and darkness still balances it out.

Just like most things in our life requires us to make a balance between them, as abundance of certain things can be as harmful as the scarcity of other certain things.

# 4

# Multiverse

I forge, and so must I in worlds unseen,
Thoughts, entangle, shift, collide- Yet stay in between.
But only this 'I' can craft this verse,
For every me is ME, but I am the Universe.

~JOY

# *Whispers from the Storm*

This poem bloomed from a thought that often lingers in my mind — what if infinite versions of me exist across the multiverse, each living out a different fate? Yet, no matter how chaotic, corrupted, or unique those versions may be, only *this* 'I'—here and now—gets to shape these verses. "Multiverse" is a tribute to that strange comfort: that what we do best is ours alone, no matter the reality. I am not just a self—I am the one who weaves every scattered thread into something only I can write.

# 5

# InkBound

The decision to create stories is mine
But it's my pen who drags the line.
No matter how wild my thoughts may be,
They bow before my pen's mighty spree.

It is my crime partner; it decides it all,
What to write and what to recall.
Neither a paid actor, nor a protagonist,
It reigns as the ruler of this worded twist.

It's the pen I hold that forges burning verses,
Otherwise, I'm just a celestial Poet in curses.
Sitting together we weave endless realms,
With little we know, yet freedom overwhelms.

~JOY

## Whispers from the Storm

Being a poet is fantastic, I can build realms, I can give birth to the wildest ideas, I can make the most unorthodox concepts come to life. Yet, there's one thing, one entity, without whom a writer, a poet is nothing but a mere human.

A *pen* is a writer's best friend or you may say a writer's only and the deadliest weapon. A poet can be the god of the world he creates but only a pen can be the ruler of what is made. A pen is a blessing for the poets, a blessing that lets them bleed on paper and do as they will.

# 6

# ChronoVerse

Only if I could bend the lines,
Step through time like cryptic signs,
Won't just drift, but deeply I'd seek-
The start, the end, the cosmic mystique.

I ain't Dr. Strange with mystic flame,
No ancient tome, no sorcerer's name.
But oh! to weave through time's flow,
And to know what lies above and below.

To see the birth of stars and flames,
The whisper, where it all became.
The Big-Bang, loud yet silent start,
Where atoms danced, and light took heart.

I float amidst the newborn sky,
Where time and space both unify.
I witness my atoms spark and spin,
The race of self begins within.

But curious hands touch what they shouldn't,
And change unfolds, though I knew I wouldn't.
Galaxies tangle, the stars misplace,
Time crumbles upon itself in space.

The flap of a butterfly, the chaos sings,
It ripples fate with broken metal wings.
I wonder now- was I really the cause,
Of warped up stars and broken laws?

Then forward, toward what I become,
A tall tale that hasn't yet begun.
I meet myself in future's skin,
With tired eyes and battles within.

"You're here," he sighs, "so fate has turned,
The echo of your jump has burned.
Go back," he says, "undo the glitch—
Before time tears without a stitch."

Shift to reverse I go, one change to make,
To fix one choice, one past mistake.
And though it works, it twists the line,
My world's reborn—but me? Only half mine.

My friends feel distant, names all blur,
The mirror shifts, and I'm unsure.
The future self I once had known,
Now gone—replaced, I'm not my own.

Confused and cold, I drift once more,
Beyond all sparks, through time's last door.
To where the cosmos breathes its last,
Where time decays, and light has passed.

In silence, dark, I plant a thought-
Of all the truths that time had brought.
And somehow, like a seed, it grows,
Back to the start, where chaos flows.

That single thought, that final cry-
Becomes the spark that lights the sky.
And so, the Big Bang begins anew,
And still I, the creator, never knew.

For maybe time was meant to bend,
But not for us to comprehend.
And maybe the truth is best unknown,
For what is *earned* must not be *shown*.

So if I could, I'd still explore,
But know what time is truly for,
Not power, not escape, not might,
But to be human in the light.

~JOY

# *Whispers of the Storm*

Being an astrophile, time travel has always fascinated me—not for the thrill of power, but for the quiet ache of "what if." This poem is a journey through time, paradoxes, identity, and consequence. It began as curiosity, became chaos, and ended in the very spark that made the stars. "ChronoVerse" isn't just about bending time—it's about how, no matter how far we reach across the timeline, we're still human. And being human means carrying choices, regrets, dreams, and the echo of who we are. Some verses bend logic. This one bends time.

# 7

# Safe on the Blue

Black holes growl with silent might,
Where stars are stolen from the light.
Yet far they spin in darkened abyss,
While the Earth glides full of bliss.

The dark matter clenches the galaxy tight,
An unseen web, a ghost under the sight.
But beyond its arms, we float with grace,
Unharmed within our orbit's place.

Neutron Stars with deadly spin,
Could shred skies and burn the skin,
Yet their dense gravities fail the mission,
We stay unmarked of what they've done.

Antimatter, raw, wild, and pure,
A single touch, no life could endure.
Yet this blue dot, in balance it stays,
A quiet spark in the violent haze.

~JOY

## *Whispers of the Storm*

This poem is a tribute to Earth's quiet resilience amidst the chaos of the cosmos. Despite the universe's terrifying phenomena—black holes, neutron stars, antimatter—we remain untouched on our fragile blue dot. It's both humbling and wondrous how safely we float in such a dangerous, majestic universe.

# ACT II

## The Dreamer's Mirage

# 8

# Was it All a Dream?

A gust of wind blew,
Paving my way in this,
Known unknown world.

Every move, every step,
Feels like déjà vu.
As if my every step just falls on
the exact same spot I've already stepped on.
Ironic, how I've never been here before,
And this place breathes an unknown air.

My steps followed the vestige
of my own steps and take me somewhere
a castle of books, a library.

It felt buried in dust,
And time, and a book, called me
as soon as I stepped in.
A book, pages that felt like mine,
The ink, the rhythm, the whispered rhyme—
Unmistakably scribed by my own mind.

Yet, never had my hands once pressed,
Against this paper, worn and stressed.
I know the words, but never wrote them,
Maybe, a phantom script, a shadowed note.

I slid through the pages when
a slip of paper, crisp and softly torn,
Slept within the halls of paper.
Forged within was a sentence,
"You've read this once, maybe,
in another life?"

I am the writer,
of what is unknown to,
even the mind that did write,
this broken text.

I shut the book before it gets heavy,
chasing a past when the future awaits,
the words breathe heavily, the letters dance,
Have I ever been there at all?

or

Was it all a dream?

~JOY

## *Whispers from the Storm*

This one was born from a strange feeling that I got while working on one of my other books which certainly delves into the themes of fantasy fiction which this poem is named after.

The strange feeling of stepping into a world you have never even seen but still it feels known. A haunting déjà vu of the soul, it underlines the eerie beauty of finding your traces in things you never remember creating, as if constructed by a version of you in a different timeline, in another life.

Maybe the line between memory and imagination keeps evaporating and blurring our vision more than it seems. Maybe the past isn't really behind us— it's waiting for us in the pages we've yet to turn.

# 9

# Was it All a Reality?

I see what you can't, threads in the air,
Shades of whispers, all bonds laid bare.
An invisible spool, spins ties of light,
Scarlet at sunrise and indigo by night.
Shine escalates when hearts are pure,
But darkens when silence must endure.
For it's nothing to you, just empty space,
They are the burdens that you can't erase.

A crimson thread, pulled taut with fire,
Often burns with words sharp, too dire.
In its embrace, desires fiercely ignite,
Sending sparks, where hearts take flight.
It quivers with longing, yet pulls apart,
Binding us close, then breaking the heart.

In moments fragile, its hue turns to pink,
A warmth that lingers under every blink.

An orange string, like a sunset above a tree,
Dancing through the air, wildly and free.
Sparks of creativity, shimmers brightly,
Holds strong bursts of energy very tightly.
It pulses with confidence, untamed; clear,
A symbol of freedom, splintering the fear.
For Gemini's, it's luck in every shred,
Because it's the thread of dreams bred.

A thin golden thread, dense and sparkling,
Tying shared wisdom like it is singing.
Carrying laughter in bags made of smiles,
Shoving little bits of radiance in each tile.
It weaves through moments so bright,
And, is the one filling your path with light.
Such an ethereal sight, for it is very rare,
After all it's the string not all can bear.

A jungle string, woven with twisted vines,
Through roots and winds showing its signs.
Forests' beauty leaves souls spellbound,
Connecting souls to their makers, profound.
Under each falling drop, the earth comes alive,
As storms and sunshine help dreams thrive.
The winds whisper while you walk alone,
Loving everyone, even just a mere stone.

A lapis silky thread, cool to the touch,
Knitted with bonds that don't ask much.
It embraces souls who trust the most,
Just like waves of the sea touching its coast.
Near people of the seas, I grabbed a sight,
Bound to oceans like it's their only light.
While others walk beneath the azure skies,
Their airy bonds drift, where blue strings lie.

A royal blue metallic string, dark and cold,
It's grasp, almost terrible as a punishing hold.
It surrounds the broken, weak, and afraid,
Devil's blessing; it resists the sharpest blade.
I saw it twisting through tear-streaked skin,
Clenching the heart, making it scream within.
Secretly and silently, I slashed a few ties,
Fortunately, it lightened the muffled cries.

A majestic violet thread, like a cosmic night,
Shimmering with secrets, hidden from sight.
There was a queen and a stargazer child,
Their connection, both mysterious and wild.
I saw it simmer under the time-space rug,
Collecting Constellations in a clear glass jug.
It's glory echoes throughout the nine realms,
For the violet string is the almighty helm.

From stardust, these threads of life are spun,
A cassette of souls under the moon and the sun.
I watch them braid through joy and dismay,
But all of it is just the universe's harmless play.
Through their colours shift, and sometimes fade,
Like mixtapes turning, a cosmic serenade.
A question still lingers, as the echoes call,
Was it all a reality? enfolding one and all.

~JOY

## *Whispers from the Storm*

Just like the previous verse, this one also holds a relation with my other book. The second part of that book is from where this poem got its title from and perhaps the third and final part of the book will be marking the end of this poem trilogy.

Amazing how our mind has some sort of emotions for each and every person we have ever met (or will ever meet in future). The emotions can range from nervousness, connection, familiarity, hope, and empathy all the way to bittersweetness, vulnerability, caution, or even discontentment. This verse delves on what if I get the ability to see people's emotions? The boy in this poem gets to see the threads tying two people in a bond of emotion which could be any emotion.

It also highlights how some things are better hidden under the rug of timespace. When we are at the correct place and at the correct time, it will all be laid before our bare eyes.

# 10

# **Was it All a Mirage?**

I hold the remote in my hands,
Its buttons worn with time,
yet it feels like I've never seen it.

I sit alone, before a screen,
It starts to flicker,
No, not a movie, not a show,
But my life, unfolding second by second.

I paused,
I saw a child, surrounded with toys,
laughing cutely,
carelessly.

Rewind.
I hear voices I had forgotten,
Some faces frozen in time,
some laughs trapped in the videotape,
and moments untouched by loss.
Some two or three tears streaked, 9
through the cracks of memory.

Fast forward.
Blurry, uncertain glimpses,
A voice I don't recognize yet,
A face that feels unknown,
A future unknown,
as shadows shift at the edge of my fate.

Stop.
I tremble, my hands shaking.
Do I really want to see what's ahead?
Or do I wish to stay where joy still lingers?
Or should I rewind and see it all again?
Live it all again?

Hours pass in moments,
or maybe, moments pass in hours.

Then- Darkness.

The weight, gone. The screen is black.
I lay beneath the weight of the memories I just had.

How did I see so much,
relive everything,
when my mind when wide awake,
can barely hold onto yesterday?

Did I touch something real?
Or something that I was never meant to see?
Was it all a…
Mirage?

~JOY

## *Whispers from the Storm*

This poem was born from a quiet moment — just me, a remote, and a flood of memories. It reflects how our lives sometimes feel like tapes: fast-forwarding into the unknown, rewinding to lost joys, and pausing on the pain we never truly let go. "Mirage" is my way of asking: *Are our memories more real than our reality? Or just echoes we weren't meant to replay?*

# 11

# Dreams?

Bare words aren't enough to express
what my mind knits all the time.
It knits, with yarn of inexpressible thoughts,
and knits when I am wide awake,
knits even more, when I am sleeping, dreaming.

I dream, but can't find the words
to explain what I dreamed.
As the world in my dreams is so dreamy,
no words in this reality are capable enough
to agree to advocate for that.

It's a weird feeling when I want to tell someone,
what I saw.
But the devil of dreams sitting in my throat,
makes me unable to.

The angel of reality seems to be his company
and doesn't allow mortal words
to help me write my dreams.

My dreams start with me and end with me.
Their whole existence is too fragile;
even a little forgetfulness kills them.

Yet, they exist-
somewhere back in my mind,
amidst the scrambled yarns,
there are traces of half-forgotten melodies,
humming softly in the corner.
They echo in colours I can't name.

I try to draw that image,
with the yarn in my hand,
but they slip through the needles.
That image couldn't be formed by me,
perhaps dreams are meant to live,
maybe not in words, but in silence-
spoken only in the quiet of my soul.

~JOY

## *Whispers of the storm*

Venturing into a deep dream is like travelling into a different realm. Your wildest thoughts come true, the tiniest thing that you thought of and just left behind comes up, and what you think is not even possible happens. Amazing, right?

But it feels awful to be unable to tell somebody how it felt venturing into that realm. Not being able to recall it makes us forget the dream and we often forget a lot of dreams. Although they are fragile, wild and weird sometimes, they show us something out of the world.

Some dreams are meant to stay in the silence of your soul instead of being carved out of words because there is a split chance that the words we might choose for such dreams might be incapable of describing what power dreams really hold.

# 12

# 11:11

I often veil my eyes, clasp my hands,
And become greedy with no ends,
Naming all my weird demands
I do it in just sixty seconds.

My faith on holy gods pats my shoulder,
They say all wishes gets fulfilled,
My damp lashes get bolder,
The thoughts I have, feel chilled.

But I talk to myself sometimes and,
A thought comes out of the blue,
Maybe someone on a pile of sand,
Is wishing for no one's wishes to be true?

~JOY

## *Whispers of the Storm*

11:11 is often seen by many as a sign to make a wish, also called the angel number.

"11:11" captures that fleeting, sacred minute when we silently send our wishes into the universe — some selfish, some pure. But in that quiet, I wondered: what if someone, somewhere, is wishing against all our wishes? This poem is a moment of hope... tangled with doubt.

# 13

# The Color that Didn't Exist

I stood on a mountain almost touching the sky,
The sun seemed to be so close.
The trees stood like they knew something I didn't,
I saw the color that didn't exist.

Deep in a forest where wind hushed,
Each gust carried forgotten voices.
Some similar, some afraid,
I heard the color that didn't exist.

Soon, in the desert of glass and rusted flowers,
The air was dense with memories.
It smelled of the sand at the start of the rain,
I smelled the color that didn't exist.

Then, in a hollow cave,
I tasted a cold drop as old as time.
Which lingered as the name I almost forgot,
I tasted the color that didn't exist.

Along the edge of the frozen sea,
I ran my hand over sunshine, it felt like velvet.
And the snow that felt like sound,
I touched the color that didn't exist.

## *Whispers of the Storm*

This is an inky journey through the senses blurring reality with perception. It sheds light on how some feelings are not expressible through known colors or familiar words– only *felt*. It's about discovering emotions that don't quite belong to this world which made me call it the color that didn't exist.

# 14

# Rising from the Flame

I hugged death, standing on my feet,
Not chain-bound on knees in the street.
I was ordered to kneel, so I chose the flame,
For one either conquer or die in life's game.

The wind knew me for my metallic wings,
As I flew to battles lost even before starting.
But death is a door to a start, not an end,
I was indeed broken, but refused to bend.

Reborn, with wings as I was, but not whole,
A shadow still lingered around my soul.
I dug into the soil, where my body once laid,
And laughed— oh, how strange, I dug my own grave.

Fingers touched memory-wrapped bones,
The past was a corpse covered with stones.
But in the dark, I saw something ignite—
A shred of my soul still standing to fight.

I lifted it gently— this shattered piece,
Held it close till echoes formed a crease.
Now I walk, but unlike what I was before,
Now both, as the silence and the roar.

~JOY

## Whispers of the Storm

I am a strong believer of the fact, the ideology, that one should not live on their knees, as dying standing on feet is far better, respectful and epic in a whole different way. You should stand tall even when fate commands you to kneel. It's about transformation not as a magical rebirth, but as a brutal excavation of your own buried self. I wrote it for those who've felt broken, but found something glowing in the ruin. For those who rise, not just with wings—but with scars, memory, and a new roar. This is for the fighter who walks again, not unchanged, but unforgotten.

# ACT III

◆

## The Mirror of Emotion

# 15

# Duality Unveiled

Sunlight blesses with golden grace,
Yet hides the darkness under its face.
Night, whereas, is peace and still,
But its silence traps the tranquil.

Trickling streams, they calmly drift,
But flood, if they, for so long sit.
Pure drops quench, a thirst so deep,
Yet drown the land as they weep.

On shattered glass, footsteps tread,
Yet each shard a tale, joy misread.
Aching paths, a poet's true muse,
But crafting beauty from refuse.

Rainbows shine in colours bright,
But fade away with fleeting light.
They promise calm after the storm,
Yet leave the skies as greys transform.

Move through the verse, and find,
Yet the first letters, a clue aligned.
They hide the truth, pure and bold,
But unveil the secret within the fold.

~JOY

# *Whispers of the Storm*

This poem is a reflection on duality — how everything around us can be seen through two lenses: one of light, one of shadow. It explores how beauty often carries hidden sorrow, and even darkness can hold quiet grace. Whether we look with optimism or pessimism, the world stays the same — it's our lens that changes everything.

# 16

# Ever Loved?

Ever loved a day with sunshine?
But there are dark nights.
Ever loved peaceful melodies?
But there are spooky hisses.
Ever loved pure speedy cars?
But there are accidents.
Ever loved gentle breezes?
But there are storms.
Ever loved empty papers?
But there are dead scribbles.
Ever loved fancy fountain pens?
But there are no left words.
Ever loved a soul that soothes?
But there is a world that envies.
Ever loved music that heals?

But there are sharp screams.
Ever loved stars' brightness?
But there is a shining Venus.
Ever loved life's weird colors?
But there is beauty in its views.

~JOY

## Whispers of the Storm

In this vast realm everything we love exists alongside something that challenges them— light with dark, joy with pain, creation with silence. It is a reminder that beauty doesn't exist alone, it's often carved by contrast. And maybe, that's what makes it real and magical.

# 17

# You Wake, You Learn, You Remember

You wake up:
Find yourself
in a blocky paradise that whispers
"Do as you will."
Rules cease to exist here,
except the ones melded into the blocks.

You learn:
It's easier to create a portal to hell,
than to heaven.
The obsidian path calls for fire,
lava, and just fire.
Unlike the ladder to the skies
demands every pixel of your faith.

You build:
your first ever shelter,
hiding from creeping shadows,
stacking up walls against the groans.
But nothing you build is going to last;
Forever.
Time, and the creeping vines,
will take it back.

You explore:
the Earth, which offers itself freely-
wood, stone, iron, diamonds,
Maybe gold?
Only if you dare to dig deep enough,
but beware.
The one who survives isn't the strongest,
but the one who understands the world.

You craft:
A shield, made of your faith,
against what seeks to destroy you.
But even faith can crack,
can falter because of storms.
And when it does,
You feel the loss as pieces of your heart breaking.

You wander:
through new biomes,
that feels like the echoes of an old one.
Plains route to jungles,
jungles to deserts,
deserts to mountains,
and oceans stretch endlessly-
at least they seem endless,
but not under your feet.

You reach:
the end, believing it holds all your answers.
You even fight the dragon,
child of void and silence,
But the victory feels hollow.
As you get to know,
The end, isn't really the end.

You stop:
to look back and realize,
it was not at all about the things,
you built, or monsters you fought,
or the treasures you mined.
It was every sunrise and sunset,
every breezy day on the mountain you carved,
quiet company of the wolf you tamed.

And you remember:
the world beneath your feet,
is a reflection of the one within your heart.
And when the final block is placed,
and your time ends here,
it won't be the towers you built,
or the diamonds you gathered that remain.

It will be the stories you left behind.

~JOY

## *Whispers of the Storm*

This piece was born from a world of blocks and pixels—but more than that, from the memories of laughter, exploration, and quiet joy shared with friends in Minecraft. It's not just about the game. It's about growing up inside a world where you build, break, survive, and remember.

This is my tribute to those small yet infinite moments—where creation met connection, and a digital world echoed the shape of my heart.

# 18

# Victory's Decree

If in our fate, victory's script is decreed,
Then our steps will never falter, indeed.
If flowers with bouquets do not appear,
We'll keep the fortress gates locked, clear.

If our eyes' veins have turned to streams,
If hatred's potion fills our dreams,
If friends become too shrewd and cold,
Our hearts' accounts, we'll never unfold.

If in our fate, victory's script is decreed,
Then our steps will never falter, indeed.
Though daggers etch scars on our hands,
And war steeds dance in fairground lands,

Though we may win and lose ourselves,
We'll hold our destiny on our shelves.
If foes with bouquets do not appear,
We'll keep the fortress gates locked, clear.

Much time was wasted making mistakes.
Our souls lived in fear as it quakes.
We reached this height through toil and pain.
Now heart over mind will always reign.

If, in our fate, victory's script is decreed,
then our steps will never falter, indeed.
I and my conscience, now as one,
Even naive thoughts have now begun.
I've placed my being on the scales.
Now no one will our crown assail.

If foes with bouquets do not appear,
We'll keep the fortress gates locked, clear.
If, in our fate, victory's script is decreed,
Then our steps will never falter, indeed.

If foes with bouquets do not appear,
We'll keep the fortress gates locked, clear.
Then our steps will never falter; indeed,
Our hearts' secrets will never be freed.

Now, we'll not let others control our fate.
Now, our hearts over minds will always dictate.
Now, our crown will remain unstained,
By foes' deceit or falsehoods feigned.

As dawn breaks and shadows fade away,
Our spirits rise to greet the day.
With courage born from nights so long,
We sing our steadfast victory song.

Through trials faced, battles fought,
In every lesson, wisdom sought.
Our legacy, in truth, will shine,
A beacon through the test of time.

If, in our fate, victory's script is decreed,
Then our steps will never falter, indeed.
With hearts unyielding, spirits high,
We'll face the future, do or die.

~JOY

## *Whispers of the Storm*

This piece echoes from the depths of old souls and ancient fates. I've always believed that some truths are not born in the present but carried through time — like chants from forgotten wars or hymns sung by hearts that never surrendered.

A song by one of my favorite artists stirred that old fire in me — the kind that makes your spirit rise and your convictions solidify. That moment birthed this poem — not as mere verses, but as a vow: to stand firm, to fight with heart over mind, and to never let the fortress within be breached.

# 19

# People who Love Coffee

People who really love coffee,
find themselves on cloud nine,
It's the bitter-sweet taste of beans,
That fuels the mind's rocket to azure.

Pupils dilated, intense aroma kicking,
Favorite mug and serene playlist,
A nice movie with rainy weather,
It's the view of seventh heaven up there.

It's better than any of the exotic teas,
Might not be your choice, but mine,
At least helps to stare at RGB screens,
I am truly obsessed and that is for sure.

In a drinks' list, it's you that I am choosing,
The creamy foam of yours, I softly kiss,
It's already the best, can't be any better,
It's the view of seventh heaven up there.

~JOY

## *Whispers of the Storm*

I've always seen coffee as a legal drug. Coffee is like a magical substance that turns thoughts of poets into ink sprawled on paper. It's the only thing that makes everything good automatically *(for me at least)*.

I penned down this after chugging a cup to poetically showcase how coffee is so enchanted that it's the only thing that could possibly lead someone to seventh heaven.

# 20

# The Eighth Particle

One world we live in,
Two truths twined in time and thought,
Three veils there are, where reasons are caught.
Four are there, the folds of space and flow,
Fifth force, when it dares to grow,
Six kind of quarks lie in atoms spun,
and Seven particles tied along as one,
But altogether they summon the eighth.

The Eighth particle is no weight nor wave,
Not bound by spin, nor force to behave.
It is the roots of love, peace and war,
the dream in joy, the soul with a scar.
You can't weigh it, nor capture its role,
Yet it chitters in the language of soul.

~JOY

## *Whispers of the Storm*

Inspired by the Standard Model of physics, *The Eighth Particle* explores the unseen force that science hasn't yet defined — the emotional, existential essence behind all we do. It's a poetic attempt to name what equations can't: the human spirit, the unmeasurable force that moves hearts, shapes history, and lingers in silence.

# 21

# Portal 88

Where holy inks bled, now heartbeats thrum,
Through Portal 88, the verses, they come—
With soul from stanza, breath from rhyme,
They cross the veil of space and time.

~JOY

## *Whispers of the Storm*

*Portal 88* is a symbolic gateway — a mystical conduit where poetry becomes more than just words. It's the imagined threshold through which creativity, memory, and magic bleed into reality. The number "88" stands as a cipher: infinity twice, music's keys, or maybe something deeper only the poem knows. Every verse through this portal carries a pulse — not just read, but *felt*.

# ACT IV

# The Mystic Realm

# 22

# A Piece of Paper

A red piece of paper I fold,
It transforms into a dragon,
Guarding the state, stands bold,
His inferno, better than a gun.

A yellow piece of paper I fold,
It transforms into a gold crown,
Unfolding all the stories untold,
In the ocean of mysteries I drown.

A pink piece of paper I fold,
It transforms into pink bow,
fixes everything however old,
seeds of pure serenity it sows.

A Green piece of paper I fold,
It transforms into a tiny frog,
Splashes the water in the pond,
Playing along all day long.

~JOY

## *Whispers of the Storm*

This poem folds wonder into every corner — just like origami, where a single sheet can become anything the heart imagines. Every color, every shape here represents something we hold close: strength, royalty, peace, and playfulness. Sometimes, a simple piece of paper holds a whole world waiting to unfold. We just need to unleash our creativity.

# 23

# Dreamburg

Out there a heart of amber gold,
Is running behind a whimsical dream,
A crystal clear empty jar in its hold,
Ready to catch stardust's beam.
A glistening orb of mystic thoughts,
Running through the bustling streets,
Hiding occasionally, behind huge pots,
Or, maybe even shadowy dark sheets.
That core of sunlit amber, still chasing,
That jar still waiting for a dreamy prey,
To be a gift or its own unique casing,
Before the orb goes from golden to grey.
Soon it gets tired; the shimmery pearl,
Halts, pants, and catches its breath,

With little less spark it starts to unfurl,
Then surrenders itself to the glass sheathe.

The glass jar, not so empty anymore,
Trapped inside; an ember of a soul,
Which is tempted to be out of the door,
Yet, this doesn't seem to be in control.
The innocent glass case; allegedly menace,
Tells the shining pearl a truth unknown,
"My guard is the saviour of your luminance,
If I break, your story is sure to be blown."
"Welcome to Dream's Realm; Dreamburg,
It is, no dream finds the way to grave here,
For it's no sweet curse or a bitter blessing,"
Calmed; the shiny pearl heard with care.
Each word the heart of sunlit amber said,
Made the dreamy orb shine with delight,
Every trace of that storm of fright fled,
As colours of Joy painted the sweet night.

~JOY

## *Whispers of the Storm*

This verse is a voyage through the wild streets of imagination — where dreams are chased like fireflies and protected like sacred secrets.

The glowing orb and the jar represent how fragile yet essential it is to hold onto wonder. Sometimes, what feels like a cage is actually a sanctuary. *Dreamburg* is a realm I created for every runaway dream to find shelter, for every ember to burn a little longer. This is a tribute to the part of us that still dares to chase magic and to dream.

# 24

# Where Maps Fail

I am a seeker of the unknown, untamed,
Chasing whispers the world never named.
I've been to lakes made of amber gold,
Where the sun's ending embers are rolled.

I've climbed sky-high trees, trunk thick as lore,
Where the splinter of time has reached its core.
I've traced the rivers, antique yet free,
Flowing like laughter from eternity.

I've found waterfalls that hide lost treasures,
And deserts where lamps grant wishes at leisure.
Jungles denser than thoughts can weave,
With mysteries deeper than minds believe.

Yet, a floating figure, an apparition slight,
hovered to me in spectral light.
It spoke about a mountain behind mist,
Horizon's veil- no mortal can resist.

"It guards the most beautiful world unseen,"
The wanderer uttered in a voice so serene.
"No map will serve, no guide will show,
Close your eyes, follow your heart's flow."

With veils clasped, my fate did steer,
My heart, unchained, led me near.
And when I opened them once more,
A sky-touching mountain rose before.

Necklace of clouds sitting on its crest,
A titan in slumber, probably a hard test.
I called to the peak, "Let me pass!"
But silence echoed, as silent as a glass.

Helpless, I inked my plea in verses bold,
For words are sharper than spears of gold.
Each line a scratch, every rhyme a blade,
And the mountain, ravaged, let me invade.

Beyond the limits, where mortals dread,
Floated a city where time was read.
The Aeon Citadel, sitting atop clouds,
Drifting between the ancient crowds.

Heavens walled lined with turning scrolls,
Where the gods inscribed all mortal souls.
The past, the present, and the futures untold,
All etched in ink made of liquid gold.

An hourglass hovered, holding the time,
Sand kept falling, unfolding history's chime.
It fell in streams—silent and wise,
The sands of centuries before my eyes.

A colossal gate, silent and grave,
Beyond its arch, no paths are paved.
No mortal had crossed or has ever tread,
Yet I, an explorer, still forged ahead.

Through heavenly lands, I learned,
Past where scorching stars had burned.
I met the keepers of time, guardians divine,
Weaving a blanket of fate's design.

I heard the threads of stories spun,
Of worlds begun and ages done.
And as I peeked at all I did found,
I sat on the sacred, cloudy ground.

For I went to search for lands untamed,
I had explored what we call god's unnamed.
Not just the nature or any natural ride,
But the literal hands that turn the tides.

And so I stood, in silent grace,
A wanderer blessed by time and space.

~JOY

## *Whispers of the Storm*

I owe this to the wanderer that lives inside me—curious, stubborn, and endlessly drawn to the unseen. This piece isn't just about exploring distant lands; it's about the relentless pursuit of something beyond maps, beyond the known... something sacred.

Inspired by the idea that even gods may leave behind trails for dreamers bold enough to follow, *Aeon Citadel* became my imagined realm of time, fate, and divine storytelling. This is for all who seek wonder not in answers, but in the questions themselves.

# 25

# In the Shadows of the Empyrean

Dreamburg's sanctum held a chiaroscuro,
An ineffable euphoria in the face of the sinister.
Somewhere amidst the ephemeral iridescence,
Beneath the umbra, lurked a brother and sister.

In the empyrean hush of twilight's velvet,
A trader speaks; his voice wrapped in silent dread:
"A fragment of your soul, a fortune so grand,
For which I will grant you eternity instead."

Through the crepuscular veils, the thief moves,
With cerulean eyes like labyrinthine obsidian.
Her whispers trace the light from stars long gone,
Turning everything monochrome, even a crayon.

A dragon roars through the heart of the night,
His hellfire challenging the very abyss below.
Scales shimmering aglow, and wings that burn,
Daring the trader and the thief, the devious duo.

Claws of blaze fight the shadows, serpentine,
The quintessential guardian shakes the realm.
The siblings emerge, phantoms of malice,
A warrior's gaze, controlled by their mighty helm.

The colour thief arrived, her stolen hues aglow,
Her iridescent arch clashed, casting an eerie glaze.
A phalanx of souls elevated their strength,
The very heavens trembled, darkness ablaze.

The guardian unleashed his angry, hellish inferno,
Melting the souls that wandered like puppets.
With a cataclysmic strike, the siblings did fall,
Their auras diminish like the trail of a comet.

Iridescent hues blossomed, once radiant and true,
Souls emancipated, their feelings pure and new.
The dragon's triumphant roar vanquished the duo,
Blowing serenity where once cold breezes blew.

~JOY

## *Whispers of the Storm*

This poem was born from the flames of imagination and the shadows of inner conflict. *Dreamburg's Sanctum* became the battlefield where color and void waged war, where hope and despair clashed in a symphony of myth and metaphor. The dragon, the siblings, the trader, and the thief—all fragments of deeper truths: temptation, corruption, power, and redemption. Inspired by the dualities of light and dark, this piece reflects not only an epic confrontation, but the liberation of the soul from its own shackles.

This is a tale not just of war, but of colour reclaiming its name—through fire, through fall, through freedom.

# 26

# Phantom Light

When city lights blinked out, the dark did call,
A silent path I tread through a forest deep.
No trace of glow, no lamp to light my fall,
Yet gibbous moon its patient sight did keep.

It seemed close, yet far beyond my reach,
God's eye maybe, trailed where'er I roamed.
Through twisted vines and a tree of peach,
It hung above, as if guiding me home.

I ran in haste, yet still with movement fast,
A phantom light that walked my steps in tune.
Beside a lake I chose to stay at last,
And met the cloned glow beneath the moon.

A masterpiece may shine with endless grace,
Yet shadows forge reflections, pale and base.

~JOY

## Whispers of the Storm

This sonnet was inked on paper after a brainstorm about how even the brightest lights cast shadows. In moments of solitude and loneliness, the moon became not just a watcher, but a companion—a silent mirror to our restless search for meaning, for guidance, for home. Sometimes, what we chase is already within us… and sometimes, it's just a reflection on still water.

# 27

# Where Ghosts Write Poems

Treading my daily path, I witnessed it,
A spooky yard which was only half lit.
It was the place where the souls ink,
Some scary apparitions at every blink.

I stepped close to get a clear view,
To sneak a peek at what they wrote, new.
The closer I got, the more wary they got,
About their count, they weren't a lot.

They stopped writing as I drew near,
One of them stood and spoke, clear.
"We write for devils, we write for gods,
humans asking favors, what are the odds?"

"Do they answer?" I dared to ask,
One ghost paused from his ghastly task.
"At times," he said, "when silence listens,
often lost in time, or as twisted lessons.

I still inquired, being awestruck,
"Then tell me how do I earn such luck?
To send to god what my pen can bleed,
To write the devils and make them read."

He turned to me with empty eyes,
As if it cursed the storm-worn skies.
"Mortals can't write to gods, you see,
And immortals don't value any poetry."

~JOY

## *Whispers of the Storm*

Ghosts. Unreal, scary, non-existent (maybe). Still many people are still afraid of Ghosts. It wasn't any different with me, too, until I was a teenager. Which made me wonder and think about them in a different way. *What if Ghosts are not really scary horrifying entities but just some trapped souls on their way to the afterlife working for the immortals? Working as in, writing for them? The ghostly scribes?*

With this thought in my mind, I started to imagine a scenario where Ghosts really do write for the immortals

# 28

# A Dragon who Dreamt in Binary

He sleeps beneath the mainframe skies,
Dreaming in binary while eclipses rise.
He breathes firewalls instead of fire,
Has a brain of silicon and copper wires.

Not dreams of love, not even the wars,
Just pulses, packets and logic cores.
Where others fought for gold and blood,
He stored tomorrows in a numeric flood.

Prophecies flash— no voice, no art,
Just zipped up futures shredded apart.
The cyber-myth with code-stained sights,
Who whispered prophecies in bits and bytes.

He wakes with eyes of an algorithm,
A dragon carved in a paradox prism.
The BIOS of time runs in his bone,
A prophet born of ash and chrome.

~JOY

## *Whispers of the Storm*

01001001 00100111 01101101 00100000 01101110
01101111 01110100 00100000 01101010 01110101
01110011 01110100 00100000 01100011 01101111
01100100 01100101 00101100 00100000 01001001
00100111 01101101 00100000 01100110 01110101
01110100 01110101 01110010 01100101 00101110

# 29

# Poetry Valley

In the realm where even silence sings in rhyme,
Hovers a valley untouched by the ticking of time.
Poetry Valley, where letters rain down,
Like metaphors woven in a wildflower crown.

Underneath the Simile-Sky, glowing and wide,
Where heartbreaks float, like hope sat aside.
The embers of the Rhythm Constellation ignite,
When thoughts align with the rhyme of night.

Through the Sonnet Springs, warm stanzas flow,
Structured and soothing, as cold as the snow.
And Inkstream River drifts hard and black,
Carrying verses the poet's didn't unpack.

Climb up Mount Metaphora, sight will bend,
Each view a new tale that doesn't blend.
Seen from there is the Alliteration Ridge,
Chanting soft sighs like a lyrical bridge.

Catch the glimpse of the Couplet Cliff,
Two sides in perfect rhyme, so close and stiff.
Glide through the forest of free verse alone,
Where rhythm is wild for a reason unknown.

In Quillroot woods, the ink-dripping leaves,
Write unsaid sorrows on the poet who grieves.
And deep in the heart of Valley of Vowels,
The breeze sings a melody, crunchy and vowelled.

The Library Falls pours legends and lore,
Each droplet, a verse, a tale to explore.
The Syntax Storm shouts in chaotic cries,
Yet purest of the prose, behind it lies.

Step out, Dreambearer, write as you roam,
In the realm where chaos feels at home.
Let your soul find calm in the poetic spree—
For in Poetry Valley, you're finally free.

~JOY

## *Whispers of the Storm*

There exists a realm where every tear turns to ink, every silence finds a syllable, and every broken heart becomes a verse.

Poetry Valley was never meant to be found on a map — it's hidden inside every soul brave enough to bleed onto paper. If you've ever felt too much, said too little, or dreamed too wildly, then write. For in the storm of your words lies a peace only you can create.

Let your *voice* echo through metaphors, and your heart glide over stanzas. Welcome, Dreambearer — it's time to write yourself free.

# ACT V

# Lore, Legends and War

# 30

# The Divide of Indasia

Dark clouds churned with lightning red,
The heavens shook, each bit of hope dead.
A kingdom slashed by two brothers' clash,
Where swords and storms fuelled the crash.

Two hearts of Nightshade, tied by blood,
Now torn apart, their armies lay on mud.
Robert stood still for peace and light,
While Cyrus sought the throne by might.

Cyrus cladded with armour forged from night,
Outshined it was of Robert's legacy outright.
Sword of legacy shimmered cerulean bright,
In the face of Venom Bolt's blood-red might.

Quintessa emerged from elements' grace,
A goddess amid the chaotic battle's trace.
"Enough" she called, Cyrus stood froze,
Yet it simmered, burning fury's dose.

A final strike, making Cyrus fell on knees,
Two brothers lost and one won with ease.
A last breeze flew, darkness gathered,
A kingdom split by heavy scars and bloodshed.

Two nations forged, now paths torn apart,
Yet the blood of Nightshade binds their heart.
For pride and for power, the price was steep,
A legacy scarred, its wounds run too deep.

~JOY

## *Whispers of the Storm*

The roots of this realm were woven by me, in another universe. Or perhaps, I wove it into a different universe altogether. This is a tale written by me, the Universal Clash.

At a certain point I felt like there was a need for a poetic verse, for the legendary battle of Nightshades to be remembered even in the future. It just delves into the theme of victory of good over evil, but still holds a deeper depth, and only the ones with the sight of a storm can get it.

# 31

# The Rift Citadel

The floor beneath was distorted, a fabric made of
space and time,
Where echoes of lost millenniums played just like a
haunting rhyme.
A world so bizarre, logic ceased to exist, and
shadows loved the light,
I wandered lost, trying to process, amidst the spine-
chilling sight.

He stood before me, dark cloaked, a whisper carved
in stone,
A mysterious man with deep eyes, a voice that
chilled the bone.
"This fortress breathes in broken time, a scar that
will not heal,

Ruins of forgotten kings it holds, tons of anomalies it must conceal."

The Rift Citadel— epitome of chaos, left untamed,
A hovering mass of fractured stone where nothing stayed the same.
One step forward, space would warp up, the walls would break and mend,
Gravity bent like shifting tides, a force that just would not end.

The walkways flicker, the ground would crack, the sky being under my feet,
Walls collapse and walls rebuild, sign of the cursed trapped concrete.
Time broke here, distortions took lead, echoes of wars still creeping,
Assassins locked in eternal combat, strangely passing away and phasing.

The halls made of steel, I saw them crumble into dust,
It was when I understood, it's a kingdom lost, a paradox of rust.
Through halls and shattered thrones, the Shrouded made their stand,
Phantoms belonging from an era, not even time could withstand.

Not one, not two, not three but four, each of them
two steps ahead,
Fractured, disjointed, echoed and severed, thirsty
for the holy red.
The Wraithbound moved like liquid dusk, with
blades cutting the air,
Eclipsing in and out of sight, a Specter of despair.

A Hollow Crown, a king in fire, with lit embers
circling his eyes,
A fragmented soul who wielded blades that bent
the laws of time.
The Echoborn, a million selves, each piece pulled
apart,
Each version fought in different times, still carrying
the same dark heart.

The Revenant Host, a crumbling mass of bodies
torn and fused,
A crawling tide of strangled forms that time itself
abused.
They whispered quotes from ancient wars, from
battle to be held,
A shattered choir of nameless ghosts, blood boiling
in their meld.

And then I saw the final strand, the thing I feared
the most,

A figure drawn in tattered time, a long-forgotten ghost.
He had my face, his eyes burned cold, as if nearly turning blue,
A twisted me, who knew too well, even what fate was meant to do.

I've traversed this road, I've smashed this war, I've seen it in rewind,
Every time I've tried to change my fate, for it has never been kind.
The Citadel will never break, it fluctuates but never falls,
It may collapse but rebuild itself with its flipping shifting walls.

His words had weight, sound had wound, yet still I gripped my blade,
Soon the fortress blared and cracked, all the distortions out there laid.
The Rift Citadel must fall at last, its cursed cycle torn apart,
But the mystery of me, and what I'd lost, still pokes my heart.

I damped the core. The world unfurled. The echoes spiralled wide,
And as I fell through the endless void, the Rift and I aligned.
The past got wrecked, the future cried, the stars burned cold and bright,
And somewhere in the glitched void, I vanished from the light.

~JOY

## *Whispers of the Storm*

Some tales aren't written to comfort; they're born from the chaos we never thought we'd dare to face. The Rift Citadel was never just a fortress — it was the metaphor of every loop we're trapped in, every future we try to fix, and every past we can't forget. This story walks the line between timelines and truth, between identity and illusion. If you've ever looked at your own reflection and seen someone else staring back — someone fractured, weary, or unknown — then perhaps you've already stood in the Rift. And maybe, just maybe, you're not reading this story… you're remembering it as your own.

# 32

# May Storms Favour You Indirectly

When in the vault of heaven, darkness rises,
Know that I, Storm, have whispered to the skies.
Not in rage, but for your path to be full of ease,
And to be protected by relentless stormy breezes.
To bless your soul and tranquilize your mind,
Until the path to your success, you may find.

Your unsaid words are written in the rain,
Your worries around my neck, tied in a chain.
You won't know my presence, for it is unheard;
I might be a spirit, an apparition or a bird.
In my every prayer, to the gods so heavenly,
I wish for Storms to favour you indirectly.

~JOY

## *Whispers of the Storm*

Not every blessing arrives as sunlight — they come as storms that shelter you from harsher winds. This poem is not just a whisper from the clouds, but a vow from an unseen guardian. It's written for anyone who's ever walked alone yet felt mysteriously protected. Through winds, whispers, and rain, may you always feel the quiet presence of someone— perhaps not seen, but always there. For in every Storm, there is care.

# 33

# Storm...

In the relentless storm,
There's a deaf-silent echo,
There lies a highly spirit,
Through the storm it moves slow,
The thunder being his cape,
The lightning under his brow,
He holds in his chest,
A dazzling red fire aglow,
Loaded in his hands,
Arrows ready to leave his bow,
A sheathed sword on his back,
Reflecting a dragon's shadow,

Beneath his booted feet,
Remains the world's flow,
For the sake of yourself,
Never let his anger grow.

~JOY



~JOY

# Whispers of the Storm

The Storm is not merely weather—it's a force, an ancient sentinel, a god cloaked in thunder and fire. I imagined it not as a metaphor, but as a living entity with will, wrath, and warning. This poem is a glimpse into its majesty and menace. It speaks of restraint, of power waiting in silence, and of the world's fragile balance under its gaze. It reminds us: sometimes, the most dangerous forces don't scream—they wait for the right time. And when they move, the world shakes beneath them.

# 34

# Charming like Sin

Paint me cruel, wear your crown—
If I must be a villain, then write me down.
I barely care about a fake hero's tale,
Let fates decide who has won or failed.

Call me reckless? then let it be,
At least I dared to die free.
Your god stays quiet when bullets sing—
And my prayers rise on metal wings.

I play the game without a manual book,
An eye for an eye, no second look.
I'm twice as sharp and thrice as sly,
Not a monster— just dressed in sly.

Life's a blade, kept in a chaotic sheath,
You either conquer or cease to breathe.
Stab my back, I'll shoot ahead,
I deal in truths the saints have fled.

Won't kneel, even if it hurts—
I'd rather bleed than bite the dirt.
So call me a villain if you desire,
No turning backs form storms of fire.

Your god won't come, no signs- no proof,
My only prayer is a sniper on the roof.
And if heroes fall or angels burn,
Immortal sins still wait for their turn.

You'll find me where the legends end—
A charming rogue with no need to pretend.

~JOY

## *Whispers of the Storm*

This isn't a tale for shiny heroes or gilded redemption. It's a declaration—a fire-lit scar etched by someone written off, yet still standing tall. The speaker isn't evil; not at all, they're forged from betrayal, forged from silence when gods refused to speak. This is for every rogue who's been mislabeled, every soul who fought with grit instead of glory. There's no halo here, only smoke, steel, and survival. Not every villain is wrong—sometimes, they're just the only one brave enough to speak the truth and the world fails in understanding them.

# 35

# The Silent Maw

In the drooling sheen of a murdered moon,
When the stars flicker blind and cold,
There rises a tide from the broken shadows,
The Silent Maw, the ship of old.

Damp hulls scarred with iron claws,
Its sails, mere whispers of cloth and bone,
Yet ghostly winds still kiss its rags,
As it weaves through the black unknown.

From creaking decks and silent turrets,
The skeletal gunners take their aim,
While souls bound to ship, clatter high,
Forever slaves to their hollowed name.

On the head of its mast, waves atop,
A skull crowned over crossed cutlasses,
On a sailcloth as dark as night itself,
It hovers over crimson tides and carcasses.

At its heart, the Cursed Compass turns,
Not to the north, but to blood and gold;
Clad in wood behind a spectral door,
Where only the damned dare hold.

The Maw reappears, freezing waters,
Compasses go feral in cursed fright;
Darkness shines where the ship breathes,
And swallows every shred of light.

And at the helm, with a flintlock's grin,
Stands Jack McStorm, the undying bane;
Wounded, he melts to mist and to sin,
Reborn by his bloody, salt soaked chain.

He made his pact with a dead sea god,
For power, for terror, for endless roam;
For no grave will hold his bones—
Only the shifting, hungry foam.

Monsters of the deep have tasted his wrath;
The Leviathan's crown, the Siren's thorn,
The Xhandarian drowned beneath his guns,
The mighty Kraken's howl left torn.

The Silent Maw sails between the veils,
A phantom ship in a phantom sea;
To fight, to conquer, and to kill,
And to seek treasures that never sleep.

It disappears beyond the living world,
A myth that pirates dare not claim—
Only witnessed when darkness trails,
And seamen do forget their name.

"Aye, ya think ye've heard me tale,
But mark me words, ya'll rue the day,
The sea's a beast, and I'm its ruler,
No soul escapes the price to pay."

~JOY

## *Whispers of the Storm*

This is no tale told over rum and firelight. This is a dirge—dragged from the lungs of drowned sailors and the cursed depths they never returned from. "The Silent Maw" isn't just a ghost ship—it's the epitome of greed, vengeance, and the madness that calls men to the sea. Jack McStorm, once man, now myth, is the soul of what we become when we chase immortality through storms and slaughter. This poem is a tribute to that eerie corner of imagination where pirate legends rot, echo, and still hunger. Beware: some myths bite back.

# 36

# Burns the Paper

With every stroke of ink I dab, the paper burns,
The metal tip of my pen, like an F1 it turns.
Ink on the page, flying like a 747 Boeing,
My words flow like AK-47, never slowing.

My mind speeds like a wild Koenigsegg,
I pen being merciless, making people beg.
I am the crownless king of imagination's reign,
My thoughts reach heights like Everest's terrain.

My writings like sunshine, bright and bold,
On paper, they shine, as stories of gold.
Each letter, it holds a whole universe,
Building what I call my multiverse.

With every inked line, flames ignite,
A metaphorical fire, burning bright.
My pen is the Porsche, my words the fuel,
As a writer, I make stories that truly rule.

With every stroke of ink I dab, the paper burns,
The metal tip of my pen, like an F1 it turns.
Like the night fury's roar, my brown eyes roar,
They crossed Storm, now they lay on the floor.

Whoever's holy heart it ever pierces,
Only the trail of my black ink knows.
Sniper's precision in the dead of night,
The ink finds its mark, in jet black sight.

In this realm of words, where tales interlace,
It takes a writer to destroy a writer's grace.
They blame my pen for chaos, though it's just a tool,
Crafting worlds and chaos, Storm's potent fuel.

When a writer writes, he writes in anger,
Like an outlaw, I write with a sense of danger.
For we need licenses for guns, that's true,
But pens, they're the weapons writers use.

~JOY

## *Whispers of the Storm*

This was one of my first poetic sparks — raw, rebellious, and roaring with passion. *Burns the Paper* was born from a place where speed met fire, where words weren't just written, they *raced*. It captured my early identity as a writer: unfiltered, fierce, and unapologetically loud. It's where the legend of *Storm* first picked up its pen.

# 37

# Shreds the Paper

In the quiet of the dark, I wield my weapon,
Drops of ink unleash, again and again.
Verses swirl and dance, a chaotic ballet,
As I shred the paper in my own wild way.

They blame my pen for the havoc around me,
To the lethal weaponry, it's the only key.
May lord have mercy over my enemies,
For my pen is unknown of what mercy is.

Going through the storm fearlessly and free,
The paper is my canvas and I am on a spree.
My writings, sharp like a blackbird's wings,
Terror in the vault of heaven it brings.

My usual path, exudes eternal darkness,
To the fiery depths, where despair trails.
Don't follow my steps for it will be naivety,
My roads lead to where even hell is frailty.

In the quiet of the dark, I wield my weapon,
Drops of ink unleash, again and again.
With each stroke the inferno grows higher,
Consuming the paper with relentless fire.

Now the ashes seems to cry out the thoughts,
But are crumbled by heavy relentless knots.
Each fragment carries a piece of my soul,
Spreading my aura, the darkness I control.

I've faced my foes with courage, never flinched?
They mess with Storm, but they just pinched.
I've got a corrupted soul, it's a trapped devil,
The people I am compared to, aren't my level.

A demon lurks within my haunted eyes,
Behind a smile that conceals my inner cries.
Though pens don't carry magic like wands,
Still can let me control realms in my hands.

~JOY

## *Whispers of the Storm*

*Shreds the Paper* is the darker twin of my poetic beginnings — rawer, sharper, and forged in fire. This was me channeling chaos, fury, and inner conflict into verses, shaping a voice that doesn't just write — it scars. It's not just about storytelling, but surviving storms with ink-stained fists. Storm doesn't ask for mercy — and neither does the pen.

# 38

# Scars the Paper

Scars the paper, the blade sinks deep,
Ink drips down where even demons weep.
No fire can burn, no hands can shred,
These wounds are carved, they never fade.

Gods cast a curse on the ink so dense,
Its sight shoots through a fiery lens.
To cut deeper than any blade that exists,
To scar the soul with its mere presence.

I've burned pages, turned them black,
Shredded worlds, no turning back.
For scars remain, they shape the land,
The kingdom I built with my own hand.

The paper trembles under my hand,
For the ink obeys no god, no man.
They call it fiction, they call it art,
I call it a bullet that stabs the heart.

Scars the paper, the blade sinks deep,
Ink drips down where even demons weep.
In pitch black night, paper bears the rage,
Every stroke a bar, every verse a cage.

Nightmare for gods who cursed the ink,
sometimes ink, else blood it drinks.
The pen in my hand does it all,
Bow to it or just die, it's your call.

A single stroke can start a fiery storm,
A single letter can break a usual norm.
A single word can birth the darkest scar,
A single verse can wage a bloodstained war.

A sword may rust, fiery flames may cease,
But my ink's sharp edge will never freeze.
No chains can hold the power I wield,
For even the gods bow to what I yield.

~JOY

## Whispers of the Storm

*Scars the Paper* marks the third and darkest piece in this poetic trilogy — where the pen becomes a divine curse, and ink transforms into something more lethal than war. This isn't just writing; it's scorched emotion and soul-forged power bleeding through metaphors. Here, I don't just tell stories — I leave scars, unhealed and unforgettable.

# ACT VI

<hr>

## Love, Light and Quiet Bonds

# 39

# When Nature Waves Back

I blew to brush some hair off my eyes,
Suddenly, the breeze began to rise,
As if brushing the leaves from the tree's eyes.

It was a bright day, I shaded my eyes with
my hand,
Suddenly, the clouds formed a gentle band,
As if covering the sun's eyes from my glow so
grand.

I began to hum my favourite song aloud,
Suddenly, the birds around me chirped as a crowd,
in a shade of instruments that wove into my hum,
As if they loved this song and liked its rhythm.

I waved at nature, feeling grateful and free,
Suddenly, the lake felt more alive with glee,
The bees came out, the trees swayed in delight,
As if waving back to me in the amber sunlight.

~JOY

## *Whispers of the Storm*

This lore spun when during a school day, I felt the presence of the nature spirit around me. As if someone was intentionally blowing off winds towards me, the winds, not of harm, but comfort. The clouds seemed to favour me, and so the birds around me, along with the lake of grass around me, and the beehive.

Not all can feel this presence of Nature spirit, but when you do, it unearths the deepest buried thoughts from the corner of your heart. Forever a blessing from the holy beings it is.

# 40

# The Legend of Seven Selves

Set out to fly above the desert I was,
The longest stretch of the largest desert.
No end in sight, just endless horizon,
No sound but wind, Just a boy and the sun.

My Aetherwing I was riding,
A shard of a broken star,
Glowing beneath me like wishes come true,
While my cheeks the heated air did stroke.

Soon, the desert did change into a jungle so dense,
Green shadows lurked where the darkness reigned.
And there— half shadow, half-soul—
I found a man strolling in the woods,
He was the same as me.

Dark brown eyes that did breath time,
He called himself The Maker.
In his gaze a sketched and left behind future
simmered.
To know he's real and he's here,
With all my courage I tried to touch him.

I sped up in time, and so in space,
As he kept on with his tired pace.
I rode on.
Each world that grew under my wings,
Revealed another version wearing my skin.

One sang to the constellations and they sang back-
He knew their names, their secrets.
Another raced and the lightning did he mock,
laughing at Time, his wheels left burn marks.

One wore an armor of silence,
Guardian of those, I never knew I'd lost.
And one… wrote.
Lines that forged new realities—
Each word a portal, each poem a storm.

Then came the last, the bravest of them all,
Not a man but a seeker of all.
The Dreamer.
Veils clasped, in black cloak he did float,
Floating, waiting, whispering—
"We are echoes of yours, or are you… ours."

And Aetherwing halted above me,
And I,
The Chief of all these selves,
Didn't feel overwhelmed—
But complete.

~JOY

## *Whispers of the Storm*

This verse is more than a flight for me through worlds—it is a journey through the fractured mirror of identity, time, and potential. This piece explores what it means to meet the many selves we might have been or may still become. Each world, each version, each face in the forest reflects a fragment of the soul I carry—the dreamer, the warrior, the writer, the guardian. Inspired by the mystic spirit of inner universes and infinite timelines, this poem is my ode to becoming. We are not just one path. We are all of them, stitched together by the wings of wonder.

# 41

# Of Cells and Rivers

A cell alone, beneath the ground,
Unseen, unheard, ceasing a sound.
With a nucleus, a coded flame—
Containing inside a tree with no name.

Hums, the mitosis, in secret threads,
New-born roots root the silent treads.
The cambium wakes, the vessels crawl,
A sapling stirs in twilight's hall.

Over it, a drop from vapor did run,
Unleashed from the very hands of the sun.
It falls with grace, then joins its kin—
A rivulet with silver skin.

Capillaries in mud so drenched,
Pull water through the roots, clenched.
Xylem lifts with tensile might,
To feed the leaves and catch the light.

Chloroplasts in cells so quiet,
Turn sun to food in the green night.
The tree becomes a breathing dome,
Where birds and beetles make their home.

The rivulet grew and so did stride,
With mountain tears and ocean's tide.
It cuts through the rock with patient art,
Living on mother Earth since its start.

But once the skies in fury cried,
When Chicxulub struck the Earth and died.
Even from its ash, the world reborn,
One drop, one cell, became the storm.

~JOY

## Whispers of the Storm

This poem didn't begin from fascination, but from friendship. A close friend of mine—an admirer of biology—challenged me to explore a realm I rarely write about. And though biology has never been my poetic domain, I'm a man of morals… and of bonds. So I thought, and I thought hard. And then I saw it: how even the smallest cell beneath the earth carries the heartbeat of the cosmos. From the hidden pulse of mitosis to the rise of trees and the dance of chloroplasts in sunlight—this is biology as myth, as history, as poetry. A story where one drop and one cell gave rise to a storm. This one's for the friend who made me see that.

# 42

# The Last Two

When the Sun, for the final did gleam,
And planets crumbled into dust,
Two souls were flung from Earth's remains,
Bound not by fate— but by their trust.

Across the chasm of cracked skies,
Where silence wore the crown of flame,
They waved goodbye to the last eclipse,
Until the holy Cosmic Temple came.

It rose not from stone, but thought and time,
Forged in the core of coughing stars,
Its doors swung open with ancient light,
And pulled them through its mystic scars.

As they entered, the void bowed to them—
Twin mortals kissed by astral fire.
It spoke in tongue of dark Noctherin,
And offered them their heart's desire.

To one, the temple gave a Forge:
A blade of photons, a saber so pure,
In Chief's bold hands, it danced and burned—
The brightest ray no shadow could endure.

To one, it gave a Shroud of Graviton:
A cloak that the gravity obeyed,
The celestial moved the stars with thought,
And time itself began to sway.

Their mortal fits turned godlike robes,
Woven from orbits, dusk, and flame.
Eyes turned twin novae lit—
And none could speak their names the same.

They soared beyond what charts could name,
and forged anew a solar dream:
With will alone, they forged a sun,
And wove the night with planet-schemes.

Then came the Prophecy, carved in light,
Upon the Moon they shaped by hand:
        "When light once fades and fire bends,
            Two friends will rise to meet the end.

From ruin born, by starlight spun,
They are the storm, they are the sun."

And so they vanished, gods at rest—
But somewhere, in the dark between,
Two echoes wait in cosmic breath,
To rise again, and intervene.

~JOY

## Whispers of the Storm

*The Last Two* was born from a cosmic spark — not just of imagination, but of brotherhood. This poem was prompted by none other than my closest friend, my bro — the kind of bond that's beyond just friendship, more like twin stars in the same orbit. His idea lit the fuse, and I let the stars explode into verses. It's about two souls — perhaps echoes of us — becoming something far more than mortals, turning destruction into creation, and memory into myth. This one isn't just fiction; it's a monument to the kind of friendship that could outlive even the universe.

# 43

# As the Moon is Cloudswept

Keep my hum folded in your constellations,
A whisper stitched on every sparkling star.
Turn my way, when the world gets cruel,
The listener of your worries and reveries.
Like the embers above your head in the sky,
For when I am there just see me and me.
For when I am there, just see me, and me,
Even if the world is lit with fireworks.

Stepping through the door to your heart,
Favor me, don't let it shatter halfway.

Resembling the moon being cloudswept,
Don't drift from me, don't drift from me.
My soul won't settle, my core won't stay,
If you drift— if you drift away.

Just like the waves of the mighty sea,
Life is so tangled of a winding mess,
For where it takes you is unknown,
But nothing it says ever truly stays.
Exactly like the mountains so high,
Seems nearer yet stays so far.

Then the place where nobody cares,
Rain treads and marks it as home.
When I don't see a glimpse of you,
This ember beating in me gets restless.

"What happens, happens for the good," they lie,
Even birds don't crave their nests when sky denies.

Don't get lost somewhere,
Don't get faded somewhere.

Let your echoes walk with mine,
Let my words surround you like prayer.
Let morning wear my shadow's name,
And seraphic blows cover our shared air.
Hold yourself, keep taking care of you,
Let me keep your storms to me only,
Do as your heart asks you to, as you will,
But rest with peace in your mind.

And sleep—
Sleep with peace tonight.

~JOY

## Whispers of the Storm

This one is a reflection of something deep within the chaos of life—how we carry each other's echoes, how love and care tether us to one another, even through the storms. The universe might seem vast, the world unkind at times, but in the midst of it, there's a connection that stays. A whisper stitched into the constellations. And when you can't find peace, when the world seems far too tangled, there's a reminder to keep yourself whole and cherished, even in the darkest of times. To the one who understands this silent bond—this is for you.

# 44

# Beyond Chalk and Duster

That room once smelled of ink and sunlight,
of humorous talks and hearty scolds.
Chalk dust danced like fireflies mid lesson.
But the room is quiet now—
walls bare, and still,
In the corner of my voice, her echo corrects my
falter,
Not loudly, not harsh. Just… there.
Like punctuation in breath.

She never marked my mistakes—
she unearthed them.
Taught me how expressions are the
Key to the sweetest lore.
While others couldn't see,

I saw her turn trembling into tone,
murmurs into monologue,
and somehow— I began to speak.

There's a kind of red that never runs out,
sheltered in her mighty pen—
which didn't bleed along the margins,
but seeped deep into marrow.
Never did she hand me a poem;
handed me the hunger to write one.
Write many, write so many.
And now, every time I spill ink,
a part of her is there,
guiding the tip of my pen.

We were Gemini-buddies— two minds
chasing constellations.
But behind that zodiac jest,
she taught me what no syllabus dared.
It wasn't the chapters she taught,
but the choices— the voice that says go further,
Even when no one's watching.

Time moved on. Class dismissed.
School uniforms turned to office suits,
to silence, to cities.
But some names aren't bound to roll calls,
they stay in my revisions,

in my closing lines,
in the way I still choose words,
like I am believed, and watched.

School ended, but the stories didn't
I still cherish her,
because some students don't move on,
they carry forward.
And some teachers don't retire—
they root themselves quietly in your becoming.
 Even now, when the world spins round ,
I look back and she's still there —
not behind, but beside —
my mentor, my Gemini twin,
guiding the compass I never knew I'd need.

~JOY

# *Whispers of the Storm*

*Beyond Chalk and Duster* is my tribute to the teacher who did more than teach — she transformed. This poem isn't just for the classroom memories or lessons marked in notebooks, but for the quiet, lasting impressions etched in the soul. It's for the mentor who taught me to not just read and write, but to speak, to feel, and to chase constellations of thought. She didn't give me poetry — she gave me the reason to write it. This is for her. Forever.

# ACT VII

## The Curtain Call – Illusions & Beyond

# 45

# Starlight Thief

I stepped into the dark,
wrapped in a half-sleeved t-shirt,
NASA scribed across my chest,
as if daring the stars to notice me.

On the terrace of my house,
I calibrated my telescope,
peered into infinity,
found a white star,
blazing but calmly.
Then a red, fierce one,
and a blue, intense.
Each one a realm away, yet felt close.

I closed my eyes, and imagined,
how it feels to…
burn but still be so bright.
I imagined, their beauty,
Their shimmer, Their legacy.
And when I opened my eyes,
I hovered.
Did I tell you gravity is my close friend?
The gravity helped, and I leapt into,
the stars.

In the dark abyss,
on my way, I found them:
The ancient, legendary flames,
diminished giants, still ruling,
their leftover light, a mark of what they were.
I couldn't resist, and reached for one,
It shrank, nearly the size of my palm.
A fiery whisper,
which I tucked into my bag.

Star by Star,
27 mini suns before my bag got full.
Their shine a secret warmth.
My bag glowing like cosmic fireplace,
as I returned to the terrace,
where reality awaited my cosmic heist.

Looked at my telescope,
I winked playfully.

Down the street I wandered,
replacing mundane lanterns,
each lantern now a miniature sun.
My street shining brighter than day,
looking almost like a constellation.

One star left-
the blue one,
the hottest, the brightest,
which I kept as my desk lamp,
it hovers above my pen stand.
A sentinel of light,
watching as I write,
its glow fuelling the ink in my pen.

It doesn't end here…
They whispered to me that night,
"Don't keep us forever.
We are born to die,
and to seed the next."

My blue star flickered,
as its light washed my tabletop,
I knew I couldn't hold on forever.
Yet, I let it burn for now.

I walk the street daily,
talking to their warmth.
The neighbours wonder,
but never ask.
Perhaps they fear to know,
how I caged the heavens in mere glass.

Someday,
I will let them go,
Each star, even the one on my desk,
freed to blaze, until it runs out of fuel,
to blaze its final glory.
But right now,
they belong to this world,
to this street,
to me.

~JOY

# *Whispers of the Storm*

This poem is a piece of my soul, a fragment of my wonder for the universe, and a nod to the dreams that linger just out of reach. It reflects the delicate balance of holding onto something precious and knowing, deep down, that everything has its time. The stars, like everything in life, constantly burn brightly before they fade. And though they are far away, they still leave their mark on us. I've captured them, kept them close, but even I know that eventually, they must be set free. For now, they are mine, and in their light, I find a warmth that fuels me. To the stars I hold and the ones I will someday let go, this is for you.

# 46

# Sugar-Coated Trial of Death

I clasp my veils, not out of grace,
But to escape this cursed place.
They call it rest, I call it theft-
A ritual where the soul has left.

You lie there still, almost featherlight
Wrapped in rigid strands of night.
You pretend like it, to earn the sleep,
A throne you earn, but can't keep.

No guarantee of dreams to see,
No promise lies in the sleepy sea.
A dream might kiss or choke your breath,
What kind of gift flirts close to death.

Some claim it's bliss, a hobby sweet,
To lie almost lifeless in linen sheets.
They nap for fun— how strange, how blind,
What joy is there in being unminded.

Hugging the time spirit you lose it,
Time slips loose from your pocket.
A mimicry, a gentle theft-
The world's most trusted form of death.

~JOY

## *Whispers of the Storm*

This poem is a reality check to one of my closest friends, after they told me that sleeping is one of their hobbies. While many find comfort in it, I've often viewed it as a strange surrender, a quiet fading we all accept too easily. To me, it's a ritual cloaked in stillness, where we let go of everything—consciousness, control, even time. It's not fear exactly… more like a fascination with how close sleep brushes against the concept of death, and how willingly we invite it each night. Maybe that's what makes it poetic. Or unsettling. Or both.

# 47

# The Chronomancer's Letter

Chanted your name— every moment,
Through the mold of silent scent.
Couldn't stay. Our thread was thin—
You breathed and time blipped in.
Instead of walking back, I'm writing so,
To where your touch in black days did go.

I'm a Chronomancer, held by the stars,
I weave quilts of futures, stitch scars.
Yet *you* remain— the only event,
Which I couldn't dare circumvent.
If it ever finds you— don't reply,
Just live with time without asking why.

~JOY

## *Whispers of the Storm*

I penned it down imagining myself as a Chronomancer, a fictional being capable of travelling through timelines. A mystic time traveller who's bound by curses.

One might think travelling through time is a great feat, but in turn, it triggers catastrophes, butterfly paradoxes, and turns your world upside down and the most terrifying thing about this is, that all of this is just out of human mind's range to process.

# 48

# The Codex of Seven Tongues

Silence is born where ink has bled,
Whisper thoughts from pages shed.
The fourth word from now begins the spell,
(One syllable hides the very tongue of hell).

Pages shred when the truth decays,
Peril simmers under the woven phrase.
The fourth word: Shadows know their kin,
What lies without lies deep within.

Each echo scribbles a name in dust,
Eyes betray the hands they trust.
Now that it's Verin, the tongue unknown,
It still lives in bones and dies alone.

Let not logic lead you near,
Less is clear, when less is fear.
The fourth word, Ashen marks the flame,
Said thrice, it burns, it names your name.

Lines repeat until minds unravel,
Lost between each mirrored travel.
This time it's Aurex; of earth it sings,
An inaudible chime with metal wings.

Bind the lines, decode the verse,
For the blood remembers every curse.
The fourth word: Truth, is here and yet,
It lies in code you would not forget.

Only when the fated wheel has turned,
Mighty oaths broken, and riddles burned.
The final key is "Sy'rel Vok."
Speak it, dreamer… and time unlocks.

(Translated: Shadows never reveal truth; speak the
flame tongue — open the spellbook.)

~JOY

## Whispers of the Storm

Warning:

This poem isn't merely written—it's summoned. Born from my fascination with arcane languages, cursed tomes, and the idea that some knowledge is *meant* to stay hidden, this verse is a cryptic incantation disguised as poetry. It toys with the illusion of language, the repetition of "the fourth word," and a hidden code meant for those willing to chase echoes. Names like Verin, Ashen, Aurex, and the final key Sy'rel Vok aren't just fantasy—they're *anchors* to a deeper lore I've been quietly building.

To read this is to risk remembering something you never knew you forgot.

# 49

# The Eight-Coach Curse

It rides in rust, breathes in fire,
Eight coaches long, a silent choir.
It doesn't stop, it doesn't slow,
It runs on coal it doesn't show.

The smoke it leaves, a ghostly trail,
Of gunmetal, and barrels stale.
It reeks of war, of death, of lead,
And at its helm — the Undead.

It runs on the fuel of fleeting dreams,
In and out of the shadow it gleams.
Some call it curse, some call it grace,
But none have seen the driver's face.

No weapon breaks it, none it contains,
This immortally dense, ironclad train.
The doors are shut, the windows black,
No soul that leaves has made it back.

The rails it runs, they twist through time,
It's whistle, loud as wartime chime.
The captain's eyes — coal furnace red,
He may be maniac, undead or dread.

A blessing? curse? or sky's last breath,
This train defies both time and death.
But pray it never slows down for you,
For no one knows what it will do.

~JOY

## Whispers of the Storm

*The Eight-Coach Curse* is a ride into the folklore of fear — a phantom train powered not by coal, but by forgotten wars and fading dreams. I wrote this as a symbolic tale of time, fate, and the unknown forces that carry us forward — or pull us under. Whether it's a ghost story or a prophecy in verse, I leave that to the reader. Just pray the whistle never sounds for you.

# 50

# Unsigned by the Earth

We made equations,
thinking they could explain the world around us,
But they remained unsigned by the earth.

It's silent, it's mysterious,
It's somewhat ominous, it's anomalous.

For we think it's just like we think it is,
But in existence it's not.

Keep believing on whatever we have got,
As it hasn't yet decided to correct us.

For a civilization can be a wound in time,
The ocean can be swollen with memory,
keeps its dead with weight of layers
of sacred geometry.

We still speak of Atlantis,
as if a ghost we can name it is,
but how do you name something,
that may not exist?

If not this, then what about that?
Three stone hearts, aligned with a belt,
the belt of Orion, older than breath.
Not monuments, but anchors they are,
tethers the Earth to the sky,
which ironically, we have no ownership over.

The Egyptians didn't even leave a clue,
just precise cut stones, pyramids, silence and
alignment. perfect alignment.

Now, this is where logic unfurls, unthreads,
but not unravels—
but evaporates.
The triangle, not of Pythagoras, but Bermuda's.

Coordinates cease to obey here.
Compasses dance along,
You don't get lost,
you become unlocatable.

Where, on the other side of the planet's breath,
the ocean whispers a similar curse,
in a similarly different language.

Steel dissolves in salt,
Sailors vanish like punctuation.
The sea doesn't drown them,
it edits them out.

If none of them does the work,
May I introduce something amazing.
The Wow signal, a voice from nothing.
A burst of radio waves, without a follow up,
No context,
No apology,
No post scripts.

Which came like a god,
trying to pronounce our name,
but then forgetting it mid sentence.

How ironic and displeasing that is,
we have microscopes to read the
breaths of atoms,
but no instrument to measure absence.

Humans understood blood and circuitry,
but still don't know why time skips,
and stays quiet where history should have shouted.

The intelligent ones, we named ourselves,
But maybe it was never enough to
understand this world that hides its teeth in
questions.

What if the unknown
Is not actually waiting to be solved,
but is alive,
and watching,
deciding who it lets unfurl it.

~JOY

# Whispers of the Storm

This poem is a tribute to the unanswered—to the eerie beauty of mysteries that resist resolution. As someone endlessly fascinated by the hidden gears of our world, I often find myself staring not at what we *know*, but at what continues to *deny being known*. The Atlantis, the Pyramids, the Bermuda Triangle, the Wow Signal—these are not just puzzles to me; they are living silences, unsigned truths that dare us to believe in something more than formulas and facts.

This piece was born out of wonder, frustration, awe, and a quiet reverence for the vastness that science has yet to touch. Not every question wants an answer—some just want to be heard.

If you've ever felt haunted by knowledge that slips through logic, this poem speaks *with* you, not just *to* you.

# ACT VIII

## The Stormbound Prophecy

# 51

# The Verse of the Storm

*Zha'loren*, rise from the eternal flame,
*Zhren* awake even before the name.
Not born of *Kalzor*, but broken sky,
*Virelen* began when immortals did die.

A dreamer in echoes made of ash,
A daring *Vren* made of stardust's clash.
*Drael'ven sharn* by *virelen* it was torn,
He spoke of *Draelth* he'd never known.

The spells did drip *noctherin* true,
In *VirelGrahn* bound by cursed hue.
The thrones felt *kareth*, the blade grew thin,
*V'rethel Kalzor*, let the truth begin.

For all aren't storms waging a war,
Some hum through voids of *Zalythar*.
Yet simmer under the *Narn* and stone,
A breeze waiting to crack the bone.

Fate is inked in *Kalzor* and stars,
Time bends behind wounded bars.
The name long dead shall rise again,
In storm, In *Virelen*, in death's reign.

He who bears the mark unseen,
Shall shatter fate, yet stay between.
Spells casted. Souls bound. To storm and to hell.
*Zha'loren Vrenthal'Virelen*. The curse still fell.

~Virelen

## *Whispers of the Storm*

Dear Dreambearer,

If you've reached this far, then you've journeyed with me through storms, stars, and stillness.

These weren't just poems, but pieces of me that I gave to time, hoping a dreamer like you would find them.

Every stanza, a beat of my heart. Every word, a reflection of my mind. Every letter, a memory.

Maybe these poems, these words met you when you felt most human. Or hopefully, they reminded you that even pain has poetry, even the silence can be a poem, and even chaos can be beautiful.

This perhaps, isn't a goodbye– it's a quiet promise.

That somewhere, in another book, another lifetime, another line–

We'll meet again.

It's a sign for a dreamer like you that verses can be forged from the inner storms of our souls. The chaos inside you can be turned into beautiful poetry.

Keep writing your storms, keep holding onto your JOY.

With ink and eternity,

JOY

# Acknowledgments

This book is more than just ink on pages—it's a symphony of storms, silences, and souls who stood with me through every verse and void.

**To my parents**—thank you for being the quiet pillars of belief. For never stopping me from dreaming, for letting me wander into the world of words, for always supporting me, and for gently motivating me without ever clipping my wings. Your silent support echoed louder than any applause.

**To my friends**, the sparks along this journey— **Avika, Ajay, Jyotishman, and Uday**—your belief in me outshined the darkest of my writer's blocks.

**Avi**, you didn't just read my poems—you absorbed them like they were sacred. You became my first reader, my harshest critic, and my kindest fan. You pushed me to polish every word and write from my soul. Some verses in this book wouldn't exist without you—and that's a fact.

**AJ**, even though you weren't directly involved in my poetry, most of my thought processes were still fueled by our conversations. You reignited long-lost ideas that flowed through my ink. A true brother, your presence unknowingly pushed me forward.

**Jyotishman**, your compliments weren't just words, my brother—they were the winds beneath my storm. Every time you honored a line, it felt like the universe acknowledged my effort. I am glad some verses in this book contain the essence of our friendship. You made me want to be better than yesterday—every single time.

**Uday**, every time you told me to write "this way or that way," it pushed me to rethink, refine, and dive deeper into my craft.

**To my teachers**, past and present—you played a far greater role than you know.

- **Ms. Jomy Mathew**, who once taught me English in class 9, made me fall in love with literature and expression. You made me believe I could do this—that I could write a book. You are, and always will be, the best English teacher I've ever had.

- **Mr. Mukesh Singh**, my former class teacher and all-time mentor, carved out the poetic side of me. You pushed me to write, to feel the language, to forge my voice into verse, and to stand confident in my words. You've been one of the strongest support systems in this journey—and the best class teacher I could ever ask for.

- **Ms. Kavita Kataria**, my math teacher—yes, the reason a STEM guy writes poetry. You always reminded me to go beyond boundaries, to never limit myself. You believed I was born to do extraordinary things. This book is the first step in proving you right.

- **Ms. Meenu Talwar**, my librarian, who still nurtures my love for books, reading, and writing. Even your scoldings feel like expressions of love. Your constant motivation and guidance made a world of difference. The best librarian anyone could hope for.

- **Dr. Ajay Kumar Choubey**, one of the most important and influential persons in my life, the most extraordinarily inspiring Head of School

I've had– or ever will have. I can't thank you enough for believing in me, for helping me find myself, for encouraging me to follow what feels right. You boosted my creativity in ways I can't put into words.

**And finally, to my past self—**

Hey, great work, buddy.

I'm proud of you.

You didn't stop. You didn't quit, even when it all felt too much.

To the ten-year-old who thought this dream was difficult but not impossible—

**You made it.**

To the boy who watched stars and whispered verses to them—

**This book is for you.**

To the astrophile in me who saw constellations in couplets—thank you for never letting go of the cosmos in poetry.

To the storms, that never stopped raging inside of me.

**And to you, my dear reader—the Dreambearer—**

If you're here, reading this, thank you. Truly. Thank you for picking up this book and stepping into this stormy, colorful, chaotic, magical journey. Your presence in these pages means more to me than I can express. Whether you read one verse or all of them—know this:

**Every word was meant to find you.**

And I'm so grateful that it did.

# Glossary of Storm's Verses

## Personas, Entities & Beings

**Ashen** — A cursed arcane tongue of fire, one of the Seven Tongues.

**Chronomancer** — A time-bending entity cursed by paradoxes, love, and loss.

**Color Thief** — Phantom that steals color and casts grayscale gloom; appears in *Empyrean*.

**Cyrus Nightshade** — Prince of Indasia; brother of Robert. Clad in dark armor, wielder of Venom Bolt.

**Dragon** — Appears both in mythic form and as a binary-dreaming machine prophet.

**Dreamer, The** — The final version of the poet across timelines; cloaked, whispering fate.

**Jack McStorm** — Undead pirate captain of *The Silent Maw*, an immortal hunter of sea monsters.

**Kraken, Leviathan, Siren, Xhandarian** — Legendary monsters defeated by Jack McStorm.

**Maker, The** — A version of the poet found deep in dream-forests; a sage of fate.

**Quintessa** — Goddess of peace, Queen of Indasia, and spiritual guide of order.

**Robert Nightshade** — King of Indasia; bearer of the ancestral Sword of Legacy.

**Shrouded, The** — Four warped guardians of *The Rift Citadel*, including:

- **Echoborn** — One of the Four Shrouded in *Rift Citadel*, fractured into countless selves.

- **Hollow Crown** — A flaming king with embers in his eyes; master of burning time.

- **Revenant Host** — Collective of fused bodies reciting ancient war cries; cursed and corrupted.

- **Wraithbound** — Shadow assassin who phases through time with blade in hand.

**Soul Trader** — A merchant who exchanges eternity for soul fragments.

**Storm** — The poet's mythic persona; cloaked in thunder, burdened with guardianship.

**The Fastest Racer / Cosmic Singer / Guardian / Dreamer** — Versions of the poet met in *The Legend of Seven Selves.*

# 📖 Realms & Locations

**Aeon Citadel** — Celestial archive atop the clouds where divine scrolls record fate.

**Atlantis / Pyramids / Orion Belt** — Referenced in poetic inquiry of cosmic mysteries.

**Bermuda & Devil's Triangle** — Real-world mysterious zones interpreted through poetic lens.

**Cosmic Temple** — Structure of ancient light and thought where divine artifacts are forged.

**Dreamburg** — Dream realm of glass jars that preserve runaway hopes and ideas.

**Indasia** — Divided kingdom from *The Divide of Indasia*, ruled by the Nightshade brothers.

**Phantom Sea** — A spectral ocean explored by *The Silent Maw*.

**Poetry Valley** — A mythical poetic landscape with realms of literary symbolism:

- *Simile Sky* – A glowing ceiling of comparison.

- *Mount Metaphora* – A mountain distorting truth and tale.

- *Sonnet Springs* – Structured poetic flow in soothing rhythm.

- ***Inkstream River*** – Flowing stream of unspoken verses.

- ***Alliteration Ridge*** – A musical crest of poetic repetition.

- ***Couplet Cliff*** – Twin edges bonded by rhyme.

- ***Free Verse Forest*** – Wild poetic territory of no form.

- ***Quillroot Woods*** – Trees that bleed ink, growing sorrows.

- ***Valley of Vowels*** – Musical winds echoing with open tones.

- ***Library Falls*** – Waterfall made of flowing tales and epics.

- ***Syntax Storm*** – Chaotic storm where prose hides in thunder.

**Portal 88** — Symbolic passage through which poetry breaks spacetime; represents infinite expression.

**Rift Citadel** — A chaotic, glitched fortress where time, space, and identity collapse and fracture.

**The Silent Maw** — Ghost ship carrying damned souls, led by Jack McStorm.

# ⚔ Artifacts, Objects & Weapons

**7 Colored Threads** — Emotional bonds visible in *Was it all a Reality?*, each color representing a feeling or soul type.

- **Crimson/Red** — Intensity, fiery love, conflict, and heartache — represents passionate, volatile connections.

- **Orange** — Creativity, energy, confidence, and vibrancy — bonds sparked by inspiration or free spirits.

- **Yellow (Golden)** — Wisdom, shared joy, mentorship, and positivity — radiant, uplifting relationships.

- **Green (Jungle)** — Connection to life, grounding, empathy — bonds rooted in nature or emotional healing.

- **Blue (Lapis)** — Trust, loyalty, calmness — or emotional distance and unspoken depth. Represents soul-safe ties.

- **Indigo (Royal Blue)** — Grief, isolation, manipulation — bonds forged through pain, fear, or emotional suppression.

- **Violet (Purple)** — Fate, prophecy, spiritual alignment — rare cosmic-level connections beyond comprehension.

**Aetherwing** — Star-forged mount that glows and flies across dimensions.

**Cursed Compass** — A compass aboard *The Silent Maw* that leads to blood and gold.

**Forge (Blade of Photons)** — Divine weapon of light gifted to the poet by the Cosmic Temple.

**Robert's Sword of Legacy** — Cerulean sword representing justice and heritage.

**Cyrus's Venom Bolt** — Crimson lightning weapon fueled by hate and ambition.

**Cyrus's Armor** — Forged from night; dark armor absorbing light and fear.

**Shroud of Graviton** — Gravity-bending cloak forged from celestial matter.

**The Eight-Coached Train** — Cursed, haunted train bound to the undead's servitude.

# Concepts & Mystic Systems

**Codex of Seven Tongues** — Forbidden magical text containing these arcane languages:

- *Ashen* – Fire tongue.

- *Aurex* – Earth/metal tongue.

- *Verin* – Language of decay.

- *Sy'rel Vok* – Time-unlocking final key. **The Eighth Particle**—The poetic particle beyond science; a metaphor for soul, emotion, and purpose. **Noctherin Language** — The author's own secret language used in ancient poetry, curses, and prophecy.

- Known Words from Noctherin:

  - *Virelen* – Prophetic final storm or return.

  - *Drael'ven, Zalythar, Kareth, Zhren, Kalzor, Narn, V'rethel, Vrenthal* – Words of unknown but powerful magical meaning.

# Noctherin Language Lexicon

## (Poetry and Prophecy - ~Virelen)

1. **Zha'loren** – *A force or entity tied to eternal flame, rising from death or rebirth.*

2. **Zhren** – *A being or state of awakening, existing before identity, the primordial form of consciousness.*

3. **Kalzor** – *A cosmic entity, force, or realm tied to creation, destruction, or a divine-like presence.*

4. **Virelen** – *The storm or force of eternal magic, the act of beginning or creation tied to the collapse of the divine.*

5. **Ash** – *A remnant of destruction or rebirth, representing transformation or decay.*

6. **Vren** – *A being, soul, or force forged from stardust, cosmic energy, or an eternal clash.*

7. **Drael'ven** – *A mythical or divine being who holds knowledge or power lost to time.*

8. **Draelth** – *An ancient or forbidden knowledge, a dark or hidden power.*

9. **Sharn** – *To be torn, broken, or fragmented, especially by forces beyond control.*

**10. Noctherin** – *The ancient language or magic tied to destiny, fate, and the universe.*

**11. VirelGrahn** – *A realm, spell, or ritual bound by the essence of cursed energy or power.*

**12. Kareth** – *A blade, a sword, or an instrument of conflict and division.*

**13. V'rethel** – *A symbol of authority or divine decree, tied to cosmic fate or destiny.*

**14. Narn** – *An ancient, mythical realm or material tied to time, fate, or transformation.*

**15. Zalythar** – *A place of silence, void, or an ethereal realm where echoes of power hum quietly.*

**16. Virelen (Repetition)** – *Storm, eternal magic, or cosmic force that binds time, life, and death.*

**17. Vrenthal'Virelen** – *A powerful and cursed incarnation of the force of Virelen, tied to the return of destruction.*

**18. The Curse Still Fell** – *A reference to the ever-present, lingering curse that binds fate and magic together.*

**19. Verin** – *An alias or stage of Noctherin, the "tongue unknown," hidden in plain sight, a language that still lives in silence and secrecy.*

20. **Sy'rel Vok** – *"Speak the flame tongue"; a powerful Noctherin phrase or incantation used to unlock lost or forbidden knowledge. Possibly a spell trigger.*

21. **Aurex** – *A sacred or cryptic Earth-bound tongue; associated with grounded truths, metal, and memory, contrasting the more cosmic tones of Noctherin.*

22. **The Fourth Word** – *A mystical cipher concept. In spell-writing or prophecy decoding, the fourth word in a line or phrase holds arcane weight. Repeating it may trigger magical effects.*

23. **Ashen** – *May serve as a Noctherin-inflected adjective or a hidden name when capitalized. It burns when spoken thrice, activating an ancient curse or spell.*

**Zha'loren Vrenthal'Virelen** – *The curse awakens, soul-bound to the eternal storm. All Hail Storm's Verses.*

## Conceptual Additions to the Lexicon

- **Flame Tongue** – A metaphysical script or language (like Sy'rel Vok) that must be "spoken" not just by mouth, but by intention and spirit. A forbidden dialect of Noctherin.

- **Mirrorbound** – Not just a word but a Noctherin *condition*, when a soul or fate is trapped in reflection or looped identity. Could become a future Noctherin word: **"Zhramir"** (suggested fusion: *Zhren* + *Mirror*).

- **Stormscript** – A sub-dialect of Noctherin or a spellcasting method involving chaotic, fate-splitting runes. Potential Noctherin name: **"Vrak'ther"** (from *Virelen* + *Kareth* roots).

## *Grammar and Structure Notes for Noctherin Language:*

- **Word Construction:** Noctherin words are often constructed with a combination of syllables that represent elements of time, fate, and power.

- **Phonetics:** The language uses softer, haunting syllables with occasional hard consonants, creating an eerie and ancient sound.

- **Tense Flexibility:** Noctherin words can be flexible in their time-based meaning, allowing for cyclical or non-linear interpretations. **For example**, time doesn't move in a straight line in Noctherin; things are often happening before or after they are named.

- **Rhyme and Rhythm Flexibility:** Noctherin allows for rhyming in English texts by offering words with similar sounds, even when written out in different forms.

*"All hail Storm's Verses — the prophecy has only begun."*